This Book Provides:

This book supports your learning of Basic Remen $\bar{Q}$ in a teacher-taught environment.

This book provides:

- A pre-course questionnaire for self-evaluation
- Guidelines for a successful online and in-person class
- An exploration of the Remen $\bar{Q}$ process
- An easy shortcut for the Remen $\bar{Q}$ process
- How to prevent a bypass and why that's important
- An ancestral method of Remen $\bar{Q}$
- Sample scripts of using Remen $\bar{Q}$
- The Rainbow Wrap Process in Remen $\bar{Q}$
- Using Remen $\bar{Q}$ as a tool and "path" in your Inner Peace Journey

Basic Remen Q̄ Student Manual

Basic Remen Q̄ Student Manual

Valeria J. Moore

Copyright 2025 Valeria J. Moore

All rights reserved. Please get in touch with Valeria at valeria@valeriamoore.com if you wish to reproduce any material in this book.

Artificial intelligence harvesting or use by artificial intelligence is not permitted.

ISBN 978-1-7371275-7-4

Published by Three Moons Publishing
Interior design by Valeria Moore
Edited by Barbara Millikan
Cover by Valeria Moore

The contents of this book should not be considered a prescription or medical advice for any disease. I suggest consulting a naturopath from a multi-year doctorate college program or a physician with a background in natural medicine before proceeding with any regimen that affects your health.

Remen $\bar{Q}$ is neither a religion, a medical practice, nor psychotherapy.

About the book cover: The cover of The Zen Tangle Woman represents many different emotional patterns. The new moon symbolizes new beginnings. This work will be a new beginning for many people. Remen $\bar{Q}$ is a new-old way of feeling peace. The day I started this manual, there was a new moon.

Contents

Introduction 1
Guidelines for a Successful Class 3
    Class participation 3
    In-Person Class 6
    Online Class Participation 8
Precourse Questionnaire 9
Class Outline 16
Opening 17
    Opening Meditation 18
        Physical Class 18
        Online Class 18
        Why do an opening meditation? 18
    Introductions 19
    Class Overview 20
    Class Goals 21
Remen Q̄: What is it, What is it not, and How is it Different from other Emotional Release Therapies 22
    What is Remen Q̄? 22
    What Remen Q̄ is not: 22
    How is it Different from Other Emotional Release Therapies 22
The Source of the Name and Its Meaning 24
What can stop your Remen Q̄ work? 26
The Remen Q̄ Process 31
The First Remen Q̄ Exercise 32
Why doesn't Remen Q̄ do it all at once? 33
Leaning-In and Bypasses 34
    Bypasses 34
    Leaning-In 36
Breathing into Presence 37

- Two More Rounds of Remen Q̄ 38
- IONS (Intention, Origin, Neutralization, Snap) 39
- A Remen Q̄ session using IONS 40
- Ancestral Remen Q̄ Method 41
- Ancestral Method Practice 42
- Scripts 44
- Principles of Remen Q̄ 55
- Rainbow Wrap 57
- Suggested Next Steps 59
- Conclusion 61
- Definitions 62

Introduction

Congratulations on taking this next step on your Inner Peace Journey. Remen Q̄ will change your non-peace reality to peace. Remen Q̄ is not new. It is ancient. It is new to this time. Remen Q̄ utilizes one of the most powerful processes in the universe to transmute non-peace into peace: intention coupled with numinous focus (witnessing the vibrational frequency of wounding through inner perception), which is then devolved into entropy (chaos). Then, out of chaos comes a reordering into peace.

There are many methods of emotional transformation in the field of wellness. The problem is that they are transforming and not transmuting. By not transmuting, a bypass may be created, which can create serious problems, such as ignoring a pain that needs urgent medical attention. Some of them require that you work with a practitioner using flawed techniques, such as digging and muscle testing*.

I am not referring to applied kinesiology. I am unfamiliar with this modality and I understand that it requires a significant amount of training and uses other tools.

Remen Q̄ gives you a method of transmuting the emotional wounds you hold without creating bypasses. Transmuting these emotional wounds as part of your Inner Peace Journey Work will empower you to:

- Claim your inner peace and the power you were born with. When non-peace happens, you will have a tool that you can use in the moment to transmute non-peace to peace.
- Feel and live a sense of connectedness to the whole.
- Acknowledge and live your inner knowing.
- Live with self-confidence and peace.
- Have relationships that reflect your sense of empowerment.
- Live consciously.
- Open your awareness to understanding.

- Live in flow.
- Experience a persistent calm and wellness.
- Create from a place of inner peace.

I have been traveling the path to Inner Peace since the 1970s. I have trained in many different healing modalities. In 2014, I found myself fatigued, frustrated and fried in the journey to Inner Peace. I was depleted. It was that state that created the opening to listen. I made the statement, "There must be a better way." I then had a knowing of the basics of Remen $\bar{Q}$. I would not embrace the gift of Remen $\bar{Q}$ for several years. When I finally grasped what Remen $\bar{Q}$ brought, I saw my reality shift in many ways toward a state of peace. I spent several years struggling with what Remen $\bar{Q}$ was. It would not be until a man in Bend, Oregon, challenged me that I would understand that this was not a binary transformation process of exchanging one belief for another, but a transmutation process of going from non-peace to peace.

This class is for the seeker of inner peace who has taken ownership of their non-peace and is looking to have a life without worry, guilt, shame, sadness, etc. The seeker recognizes the wisdom of Remen $\bar{Q}$. This class is not for someone still looking outside themselves for answers.

The book and class are designed to teach you Remen $\bar{Q}$ so you can use it as a tool for the transmutation of your non-peace.

The teacher has the autonomy to switch things around as they think is necessary.

Guidelines for a Successful Class
(Please read before class)

Class participation

Breaks: Be on time when returning from breaks. Breaks are essential to learning this Inner Peace Journey work. Stepping away from the practice (breaks) facilitates an opening for the flow of information. It clears our focus for a few minutes and allows new information to flow.

Use only Remen $\bar{Q}$: Many people coming to this class are familiar with other modalities. You are here to learn Remen $\bar{Q}$. Please refrain from using other modalities during class.

Respect: Please be respectful of others. Your peers come from a variety of backgrounds and hence have had a broad spectrum of experiences.

Do only Remen $\bar{Q}$ and as it is taught. Deviation from the instruction could create additional work for the teacher. The intention is peace and only peace. If an intention other than peace is inferred, it will not resolve. In one instance, a person set an intention other than peace, and they experienced swirling until they contacted me 3 days later. The situation was resolved by using the swirling as the non-peace and doing $\bar{Q}$. Remen $\bar{Q}$ will only resolve when the intention is peace.

Participate in the exercises. There is a pre-course questionnaire following this chapter. If you have trouble with any of the exercises in the questionnaire, please let your teacher know in advance. Your teacher will advise you. This work is about learning to know your heart and trusting the information you receive. You may not always feel a contraction in your heart, but you have a limiting pattern you know you need to transmute.

During class, I ask that you not use pendulums, tarot decks, muscle testing, channeling, etc. You are learning to trust your heart's inner wisdom. If you have difficulty accessing your heart's feelings, pay attention to your body. Does your body present you with contractions(non-peace)? If so, use that as your point of non-peace. *(Suggestion: start journaling this before class.)*

Use your journal to keep track of your Remen Q̄ work during class. Your teacher will guide you in this process.

If you need additional assistance, consider scheduling an appointment with your teacher after class for continued support.

Class is a "story-free" zone. We all have a story of our wounding, and your story is important. In class, do not share your wounding story. If you need to get it out, journal the story and then use Remen Q̄ to transmute the wounding and the story to peace. The teacher will show you how.

Remen Q̄ is a solitary exercise, so there is no need to work with another student. Your journal will be your confidante and witness. Your teacher will guide you through the exercises until you can use the acronym IONS[1].

Remen Q̄ is not a religion, psychotherapy, or medical practice.

Disruptive Behavior. You may be removed from class for inappropriate behavior, including but not limited to the use of alcohol or non-prescription drugs that alter your judgment; disrupting class instruction; violating the class guidelines; disrespecting another; violent behavior; bullying; etc. No refund or class credit will be given for removal from a class for inappropriate behavior.

---

[1] Moore, Valeria (2021). *The Remen Q̄ Method: An Easy Do-It-Yourself Process to Create Inner Peace and Change Your Reality*, pg. 3. Keizer, Oregon, USA. Three Moons Publishing.

Medications. If you are taking medications that alter your perception of your body or feelings, please consult with your instructor before enrolling in the class.

In-Person Class

Fragrances: Fragrances are prohibited.

Cell phones: Cell Phones should be set to airplane mode. Even the sound of a vibrating phone can be jarring if you're in a Remen $\overline{Q}$ session.

Do not talk to others during the class exercises or during instruction. This work is a meditation, and you will cause a break in the work of others. Your teacher will guide you to times for questions and comments.

Arrive on time for class. Please send a text to your teacher before class starts if you will be late, and give your time of arrival. Teachers will often hold the start of a class if it is only going to be a few minutes. There is an opening meditation at the beginning of the class that should not be interrupted. The teacher may ask you to wait before entering the room.

If you are physically ill, do not come to an in-person class. Instead, please get in touch with your teacher as soon as possible to inform them that you will be unable to attend. If you are capable, perhaps a Zoom call could be set up so you can still attend the class. If not, arrange with the teacher to retake the class.

What to bring to class
- Kleenex
- Layered clothing (a sweater, hoodie or jacket)
- A journal, pen or mechanical pencil
- Your copy of the Remen $\overline{Q}$ book and this student manual.
- Water. I urge you to stay hydrated.
- Snacks.

Emotional Release - Crying

Below are some guidelines to follow while in class:

1. Do not trivialize crying.

2. Do not offer platitudes (for example, "Let it go," "This will pass," or "Get over it," etc.). Platitudes reinforce existing wounds and may create new ones. Platitudes are also a way of disconnecting from another person's emotions.

    Additional platitudes that harm people:

    - *You'll be fine*
    - *This will pass*
    - *Get over it*
    - *Everything happens for a reason*
    - *Time heals all wounds*
    - *Just look on the bright side*
    - *What doesn't kill you makes you stronger*
    - *Someone has it worse than you*
    - *It could be worse*
    - *Be positive, and it will happen*
    - *Suck it up*

3. Do not stop someone from crying by offering a Kleenex.

4. Do not touch the student. Touching the student will break the release they are going through and may send the message that their crying makes you uncomfortable. This contact would have the effect of making them feel invalidated. You have been taught to offer hugs or a Kleenex when someone is crying. As a society, we have also been taught to "suck it up." When someone is crying, it makes us uncomfortable, and we want to "fix it" or "make it go away."

Online Class Participation

Work out the technology bugs before class. Zoom offers a free account. Set up an account, test your equipment and become familiar with the screens. Show up at least 15 minutes before the start of class.

What to do if you become physically ill: If you are physically ill, get in touch with your teacher as soon as possible to inform them that you will be unable to attend. You and your teacher will work out a time to retake the class.

Cell phones: Cell Phones should be in airplane mode. Even the sound of a vibrating phone can be jarring if you're in a Remen $\bar{Q}$ session.

If possible, have a quiet, dedicated space for your class participation. Any extraneous noise can disrupt the flow of the class. You will probably be kept on mute most of the time, but visual disturbances, pets, children, etc., can disrupt the energy of attention.

Precourse Questionnaire

Remen Q̄ is a focused personal endeavor. In this class, you will only work with the teacher. Please let the teacher know if you have difficulty with inner reflection, journaling, and feeling your heart or body information. These are areas of non-peace that can be addressed with Remen Q̄. You may not have time during class to address all blocks. However, your teacher can guide you in the Remen Q̄ work needed to transmute limiting non-peace and the basic tools necessary for your Inner Peace Journey.

Below is a self-evaluation questionnaire that helps you focus on your intent for taking the class. The teacher may use only part of this questionnaire or develop their own questions. The teacher may send you a pre-course questionnaire after registering for the course.

You can use this questionnaire for your own evaluation.

1. Do you have the Remen Q̄ class guidelines that your teacher sent (the teacher may choose to use these questions)? Are you willing to adhere to those guidelines? If not, what is holding you back? Please contact the teacher if you have any difficulty with the guidelines. (This would also apply to the suggested guidelines in the prior section.)

_____
_____
_____
_____
_____

2. What are your emotional goals for taking this class?

_____
_____
_____
_____
_____
_____
_____

3. Do you have relationships with others that are non-peace? Are you willing to own your non-peace relationship? If not, why?

_____
_____
_____
_____
_____
_____
_____

4. What support do you believe would help you achieve your emotional goals?

_____
_____
_____
_____
_____
_____
_____

5. Journaling is a vital component of the Inner Peace Journey. Do you currently keep a journal? If not, do you have difficulty journaling? Let your teacher know if you have difficulty with journaling. What stops you from journaling? The teacher can guide you through transmuting those blocks.

_____
_____
_____
_____
_____

6. Are you willing to take responsibility and ownership for how you feel related to an emotional wound? If not, what stops you?

_____
_____
_____
_____
_____

7. If you believe you have a numb heart, are you open to transmuting the numbness? If not, what stops you? How does having heart numbness serve you? Are you willing to transmute the benefit (which is non-peace) to peace?

_____
_____
_____
_____
_____
_____

8. Are you willing to connect with the feelings in your body so you can transmute your wounding? If not, what stops you? How does it benefit you to **not** transmute the block to feeling your body? Are you willing to transmute that benefit (non-peace) to peace?

_____
_____
_____
_____
_____
_____

9. Are you willing to transmute self-sabotage—examples: overthinking, procrastination, not taking responsibility, creating chaos, overly strong boundaries, etc? If not, why? What do these states of non-peace do for you?

_____
_____
_____
_____
_____
_____

10. Do you want to focus on a particular problem during this class? What is the particular issue causing non-peace?

_____
_____
_____
_____
_____
_____

11. Are there any concerns you might have about this class?

_____
_____
_____
_____
_____
_____

12. Do you feel like you can have peace in your life? If not, why?

_____
_____
_____
_____
_____
_____

13. Do you have trouble staying focused? Explain.

_____
_____
_____
_____
_____
_____

14. Are you open to change in your life? If not, how does not changing serve you?

_____
_____
_____
_____
_____
_____

15. Do you have any physical problems? And do you think there is an emotional component to the physical problems? If so, what is it?

_____
_____
_____
_____
_____
_____

16. Do you deserve peace? Do you know what peace is?

_____
_____
_____
_____
_____

Class Outline*

The teacher may modify the class outline provided below. This outline provides a recommendation and general approach for the class.

1. Opening
2. Remen Q̄: What is it, What is it not, and How is it Different from other Emotional Release Therapies?
3. Source of the name and its meaning
4. What can stop your Remen Q̄ work?
5. The first Remen Q̄ exercise
6. Why doesn't Remen Q̄ do it all at once?
7. Leaning in/Bypasses
8. Breathing into Presence
9. Two more rounds of Remen Q̄
10. IONS (Intuition, Origin, Neutralization, Snap)
11. A Remen Q̄ session using IONS
12. Ancestral Remen Q̄ Method
13. Ancestral Method Practice
14. Scripts
15. Principles of Remen Q̄
16. Rainbow Wrap (optional)
17. What can stop your Remen Q̄ work?
18. Suggested next steps
19. Conclusion

Opening

Opening Meditation

Physical Class

Your teacher will guide you through this opening meditation. The teacher will instruct you to hold hands in a circle, holding hands with palms facing palms. Breathe into Presence. Close your eyes and imagine a ball of white light at the center of the circle. Then imagine a ray of that same light extending from your heart to the ball of light. Then, visualize the ball of light expanding and encompassing the circle. Then the ball of light expands out across the planet and the universe. The teacher will then softly break the connection. The ball of white light represents the one universal heart.

Online Class

Your teacher will walk you through the opening meditation. The teacher will ask you to Breathe into Presence, close your eyes, and imagine a ball of white light about 3-5 feet in front of you, along with a ray of light extending from your heart to the ball of light. Imagine you are connected to the ball of light by a ray of light from your heart. Then, visualize the ball of light expanding and encompassing the virtual circle. Then, visualize the ball of light expanding across the planet. Stay in that space for approximately five breaths and then the teacher will softly break the connection. The ball of white light represents the one universal heart.

Why do an opening meditation?

Meditation quiets the mind, allowing thoughts about your life outside the class to subside and bring you into a state of presence.

Meditation fosters an increased awareness of bodily sensations and emotions as they emerge. This state of awareness is an essential aspect of the work you will be doing with Remen $\overline{Q}$. You will be checking in with your heart or body to monitor the progress of your exercises.

Introductions

Please keep your introduction brief.

Your teacher will give you a list of topics(see below) to address as part of your introduction. The suggested list may differ from your teacher's.

- Name
- Where are you from?
- How did you hear about Remen $\bar{Q}$?
- Have you used Remen $\bar{Q}$?
- What are your expectations for the class?

Class Overview

You will learn:

- The Remen $\bar{Q}$ method
- The Remen $\bar{Q}$ IONS method
- Ancestral Method of Remen $\bar{Q}$ method
- About bypasses and leaning-in
- Principles of Remen $\bar{Q}$
- What can hijack your Remen $\bar{Q}$ session

Class Goals

After completing this class, you should know:

- How to do a Remen Q̄ session.
- How to and when to lean-in.
- When you have completed your Remen Q̄ session on an issue without creating a bypass.
- How and when to do the ancestral method.
- Why Remen Q̄ is a transmutation and not a transformation.
- Why transformation processes create bypasses.
- That Remen Q̄ can become integral to your Inner Peace Journey.
- How to use the Rainbow Wrap (optional).
- What can stop your Inner Peace Journey?

Remen Q̄: What is it, What is it not, and How is it Different from other Emotional Release Therapies

What is Remen Q̄?

1. A method of **transmuting** non-peace to peace.
2. An ancient process that parallels the Essene and Egyptian practices.
3. A method for harmonizing energy systems that impact the entire system.
4. An intention of peace.
5. Heart-based, which is the portal to your soul's wisdom
6. Expansion into our natural state of being.
7. Completed by you in minutes; no need for additional support.
8. Multi-dimensional
9. It is an elemental tool in an alchemical approach to the Inner Peace Journey Work.

What Remen Q̄ is not:

1. A religion, medical practice or psychotherapy.
2. A method of **transformation**.
3. A bypass when done thoroughly.
4. Story-based (Reinforces trauma when the story is told).

How is it Different from Other Emotional Release Therapies?

1. No digging (which can be endless and inaccurate). *See Definitions page 64 for an explanation of the term 'digging'.*

2. No muscle testing (which can be inaccurate). *See Definitions page 69 for an explanation of the term 'muscle testing.'*
3. It does not create additional bypasses (which can cause unwellness). *See page 62 for more information on bypasses.*
4. Has a process for transmuting existing bypasses.
5. Transmutes, which raises you to a higher state of peace and harmony.
6. You don't need to know the origin.
7. You don't need to tell a story (this just reinforces the trauma).
8. It makes a big difference in how happy and fulfilled you feel.

The Source of the Name and Its Meaning

Every aspect of the name Remen Q̄ has meaning. The word Remen is the name of a hieroglyph. The hieroglyph, as described by Egyptologists, is a measurement; however, the Ancient Egyptians were more than we could have imagined.

The following few paragraphs are copied from <u>The Remen Q̄ Method: An Easy Do-It-Yourself Process to Create Inner Peace and Change Your Reality.</u>

> ***Remen was not a linear measurement as has been theorized by Egyptologists.*** *The ancients understood that 'remen' was a measurement of our universe's multi-dimensional dynamic nature and its translation across dimensions. Remen was an understanding of the multiplicity effect of energy as it moved across dimensions. Remen is a conceptual measurement that shifts its quantification by the dimensional awareness present. In 9-dimensional awareness, an energetic quantification is different from what would be experienced in 4-dimensional awareness.*
>
> *'Q' was a nod to our god nature. Q was an 'extradimensional' race of beings in the Star Trek TV series and movie. The Q race had many god-like qualities, and among those was the ability to change reality. The Q character, near the end of the series, became a mentor to the humans. A human could join the Q Continuum by evolving and changing their DNA programming if chosen by the Q Continuum. This alteration created an ascension to a higher non-human life form that did not require a physical body.*

The bar or vinculum over the 'Q' in mathematical terms is placed over a set of numbers to represent their infinite repetition. In mathematical terminology, it is used to designate the repeating nature of a set of decimal numbers. In Remen, the vinculum acknowledges the infinite nature of awareness. [2]

Remen $\bar{Q}$ is a process that transmutes limiting patterns -- of fear and contraction -- to peace. Our human existence on this planet is marked by fear or a lack of peace. Fear is a contraction of the flow of life force, energy of a certain quality. When fear transmutes to peace, there is an effect across dimensions. Energy releases to continue flowing. The expression of that energy can be quantified, and that is Remen. The transmutation of fear into peace releases a pulse of energy that, as it flows across the dimensions, creates a transmutation in relationships that are fields of awareness, information and knowing. As you make these changes, you also alter our DNA and, consequently, your physical being. You transmute the emotional wounding held in epigenetic tags on our DNA. You change the reality of all. The effect of this transmutation is infinite.

---

[2] Moore, V. (2021). *The Remen $\bar{Q}$ Method: An Easy Do-It-Yourself Process to Create Inner Peace and Change Your Reality*, Viii. Keizer, Oregon, USA. Three Moons Publishing.

What can stop your Remen Q̄ work?
(and your Inner Peace Journey)

The list below of limiting patterns may block your journey to Inner Peace. You may sense these limiting patterns as a feeling of being stuck. You may feel stuck in your job or a relationship. You may feel like you lack creativity. You may have a sense that nothing is moving in your life, and you're repeating the same old, dry, lifeless patterns. Your life may feel and look grey, with no real color; that is a metaphor for the flow of life. You feel your life is stagnant.

If any of the points listed below resonate, I suggest you take the opportunity afforded in this class to begin transmuting these wounds.

- **Not trusting your heart.** Your Inner Peace Journey starts with you transmuting the wounds of your heart and trusting yourself. Your heart is the bridge to the wisdom of your soul. In peace, your heart knows a wisdom that is sacred and informs your Inner Peace Journey. Without transmuting the lack of heart trust, everything you do will be informed by the mind or body, not the heart. It will be incoherent.

- **Heart numbness**. You may not feel the contraction of non-peace because you have numbed it out. A numbed heart impairs the flow of life force and may stop you from transmuting limiting patterns because you don't feel the non-peace.

   The use of some drugs may also numb your ability to feel emotions.

   The material in the following paragraph is excerpted from the upcoming book Creating a Foundation for Inner Peace. The book is scheduled for release in late 2025 or early 2026. You can check https://peacealchemist.com for updates.

Someone emotionally devastated will create a filter, a heart numbness, which becomes a boundary. That boundary stops emotional experiences, both pleasant and unpleasant. As a consequence, the student has no feedback from their heart. **They may have created numbness in their heart so that they no longer feel the pain of non-peace.** *Numbness of heart feelings is a state of non-peace. When they numbed their heart's feelings, they traded one non-peace state for another.* **Despite their heart numbness, their body lets them know they are carrying states of non-peace.**

- **Unwilling to work with a journal**. It is suggested, in the Remen Q̄ work, to use a journaling process to track your work. *When you journal, you listen to your heart's transmission of wisdom beyond your logical thinking processes. Journaling allows you to focus your thoughts and yields insights into the limiting patterns you may be holding.* * In the Scripts chapter, later in this book, several examples are provided to illustrate how your journaling may flow.

  *Statement is from a book I am currently writing, <u>Creating Foundations for Inner Peace</u>.

  I have known people who refuse to write even a simple email. The idea of using a journal to hold their heart's feelings and ideas induces fear. Writing in their past made them vulnerable to judgment, humiliation and exposure, and most often, that judgment was harsh criticism from a teacher or parent.

- **Ignoring the subtle and sometimes not-so-subtle clues your body gives you**. Your body will tell you when there is non-peace. Non-peace can manifest as body pain or contraction. A contraction can manifest as stress, a headache, pain, etc. You may have developed skills that allow you to ignore the contraction in your heart or the pain in your shoulders, for example. However, ignoring these messages from your body and higher self can hinder your progress on your Inner Peace Journey.

- **The use of tarot, spiritual bypasses, psychic readers, muscle testing, pendulum, etc., as a crutch**.

    When you use tools or other people to inform your life journey, you are not transmuting the wounds or activating and developing your intuitive skills. One of the critical elements of this journey is **trusting** *yourself. The use of these tools becomes a spiritual bypass. However, besides creating a spiritual bypass, they may also be inaccurate.*

    The use of a pendulum moves you away from accessing your higher wisdom. You rely on a tool instead of trusting your inner voice or knowing. Pendulum use is not always accurate. According to the training I received, using a pendulum is based on your mind state at the time of use. I have found that the results obtained using a pendulum are no better than those of random chance. Others have found that the pendulum is highly accurate for them.

    Muscle testing is based on the idea that your muscles will either strengthen or weaken when a statement is made. The muscles are tested for strength when a statement is made to determine its truth to you. One method involves pressing your forefinger and thumb together, and a healing practitioner holds your forefinger with one hand and your thumb with the other. As you make a statement, the healing practitioner will easily pull your fingers apart if the statement is false. Or, using both hands, you make interlocking circles with your thumb and forefinger pressed together; when a statement is made, you pull the fingers apart and break the circles. The supposition is that your muscles will weaken, and your fingers will pull apart easily if the statement is false. The problem is that fingers can develop diseases that weaken them, for example, arthritis. If your blood chemistry is out of balance, the muscle testing will be incorrect. If you are dehydrated, the muscle test will be inaccurate. If you are emotionally distraught, the muscle testing will be incorrect. Additionally, I have encountered instances where people have manipulated the test results. Several scientific studies have evaluated the validity of muscle testing, and the results indicated that muscle testing was no better than random chance.[3]

- **Thinking you can hack the process by setting an intention other than peace.** The intention is ALWAYS peace and only peace. There are no shortcuts. Setting an intention other than peace will not resolve.

- **Not owning a relationship** that is non-peace. For example, when you take a new job, a coworker treats you with disdain and mistrust on the very first day. The coworker is in fear of losing their job. Although you were not the cause of the coworker's fear, that is the relationship that exists between you. To transmute this uncomfortable work situation, you must take ownership of the relationship. You feel your coworkers' non-peace toward you, and you may feel non-peace toward them. That is the relationship.

- **Unwilling to transmute self-sabotage**—examples: overthinking, procrastination, self-doubt, creating chaos, overly strong boundaries, etc. You may think you are keeping safe by engaging in these behaviors, but these behaviors can hinder the flow of life force and be fear-based.

- **Loss of Focus.** When I work on myself, I occasionally find myself thinking about another topic. I would forget what I was working on. There was a secondary gain to keeping the wounding, and I would steer myself away from the work. To address this, you would Remen Q̄ the loss of focus as the non-peace. Then, go back and do the initial transmutation work. Journaling will keep you on track when you find yourself losing focus.

---

[3] Moore, Valeria. (2024) *Alchemy of the Third Eye and Pineal Gland: Healing Your Intuition*, 76. Keizer, Oregon, USA. Three Moons Publishing.

- **Needing to know the origin.** You may have difficulty getting a perception of the origin. You don't need to know the origin. Create something (for example, a blue vase) or use one pre-determined image throughout the witnessing of the origin. Whatever you perceive will have a vibrational match with the origin.

- **You use your wounding to stay safe.** For example, wanting to control the outcome. If you feel that not being in control is too dangerous, are you willing to Remen $\overline{Q}$ the fear of being hurt or not in control?

The Remen Q̄ Process

Bring into your awareness a non-peace that you hold. Feel it in your heart. If you have trouble feeling non-peace but you know you have it, proceed with that awareness. Or, if you feel it in your body, you can use that as your non-peace. For example, you may carry stress in your shoulders, and they feel tight. That is non-peace.

Close your eyes and place your fingertips on your heart space. Then, breathe into presence by taking five slow, deep breaths through your nose and out through your nose without pausing, using tummy breathing.

1. **I am witness to the field of intention to neutralize this created pattern.** *(Say this in your inner voice.)*

2. **I am witness to the origins of this created pattern.**
   (Say this in your inner voice and visualize a representation of the origin.)

3. **I am witness to the neutralization of this created pattern.** *(Say this in your inner voice and visualize a change in the image. Halfway through visualizing the change, **snap** open your eyes.)*

4. Move your attention to your body and watch until you feel it is complete. *(If there is a sensation of lightheadedness or swirling, allow the sensation to finish.)*

The First Remen Q̄ Exercise

There are three "long" Remen Q̄ exercises in this class and your teacher will guide you through them. Then, you will be able to do the IONS version (short version) of Remen Q̄, which is described later in this guide. Later in this guide, you will find scripts that provide additional clarity to the process.

A sample process for a Remen Q̄ process:

Possible issue: *My mother criticizes everything I do.*

You: *Where do I feel this in your body? My heart.*
(Record your response in your journal.)
How intense is the contraction in your heart? 8 out of 10
(Record your response in your journal.)

The teacher will guide you through Breathing into Presence and the Remen Q̄ steps in the prior chapter.

You: *When you feel complete, check the level of contraction and intensity.*

Checking in*: The contraction is now a 2. (More Remen Q̄ is needed. Record your response in your journal.)*

If you have not reached calm and peace in your heart, you will need to lean-in, as explained on page 36, and do more rounds of Remen Q̄.

Why doesn't Remen Q̄ do it all at once?

The following two paragraphs are from <u>The Remen Q̄ Method: An Easy Do-It-Yourself Process to Create Inner Peace and Change Your Reality</u> on page 76.

> ***Remen Q̄ does not clear a specifically created pattern to be replaced with another created pattern****. For example, you experience not feeling good enough. Your heart contracts, and you enter a state of non-peace. In that state of non-peace, you may experience shame, humiliation, and wanting to hide. There are many patterns of non-peace within this one experience. With Remen Q̄ you set the intention for peace, and after doing the Remen Q̄ process, maybe multiple times, you feel calm and neutral. The feeling of not being good enough, shame, humiliation, and wanting to hide has been changed to the possibility that has the highest probability at that moment for peace.*
>
> ***You may find that in the future, you may need to address a feeling of non-peace again****. That feeling may have the same label, but it is not the same created pattern transmuted in the past. Starting a practice or 'a way' of self-reflection, journaling, meditation, and using Remen Q̄ are helpful in the journey to peaceful awareness. This practice offers you the opportunity to explore the non-peace that has not yet risen into your conscious awareness[4].*

---

[4] Moore, Valeria. (2021). *The Remen Q̄ Method: An Easy Do-It-Yourself Process to Create Inner Peace and Change Your Reality*, pg 76. Keizer, Oregon, USA. Three Moon Publishing.

Leaning-In and Bypasses

Bypasses

When working with Remen Q̄ you are working with non-peace that is transmuted to peace. You may be working with a feeling of non-peace that centers around a specific issue. For example, 'I'm not good enough.' This state of non-peace likely stems from your childhood (or perhaps your ancestral past), and you have probably experienced that feeling hundreds of times by the time you started doing Inner Peace Journey Work. Each time you experience this emotional wound, you create a new emotional wound. A vibrational frequency is composed of your experience and awareness in the moment. When a state of non-peace is similar enough to another non-peace's vibrational frequency, transmutation will likely occur. Otherwise, additional Remen Q̄ will be necessary and a session should always be checked per the leaning-in method given in this chapter.

When you partially transmute a state of non-peace to peace, you have created a bypass. When you use a '**transformation**' modality to 'heal' (this includes conventional medicine) a malady or 'clear' an emotional wound, you have created a bypass. For example, you have gall bladder surgery to remove a diseased gall bladder, but you do not address the emotional wounds that crystallized and created the diseased gall bladder. You **bypassed** the need to address long-held feelings of bitterness that may have been the progenitor of the gall bladder disease. **A bypass is a state where you believe you have released or cleared a state of non-peace, only to discover later that the change was temporary**. This misbelief can cause a person to delay seeking appropriate care in a timely manner, which could have serious consequences. Discovering you have a bypass can lead a person to believe they have been betrayed and deceived, setting up another emotional wound. A bypass may not be evident for many years. In the case of the diseased gall bladder patient, the bitterness may appear in another part of the body as a new malady.

Bypasses may also develop as a consequence of giving up your agency to another (person, god, shaman, priest, doctor, healer, entity, modality, institution, etc.) so you can abrogate your responsibility and will. Giving up your agency allows you to blame someone or something else for harm or failure, and you can then play the victim. You have given up your authority so you don't have to take responsibility, and in so doing, you perpetuate a state of victimhood.

Leaning-In

Leaning-In is the name I gave the body check-in you do after having done a Remen Q̄ session. I place my hand on my heart and lean forward a small amount. I did this instinctively one day, hence the label 'leaning-in.'

Leaning-in is done by placing your hand on your heart and recalling the original state of non-peace. If the perceived wounding is ghost-like or not present, and there is a feeling of peace, calm or neutral, then you are complete. If there is still non-peace, the contraction may be subtle. It could be an uneasy feeling or maybe a flat feeling.

Additionally, recall an episode of experiencing the non-peace you are working on, and if it is present and clear in your memory, whether you feel it or not, then there is more work to do.

Leaning-In Exercise

Go back to your prior Remen Q̄ sessions in this manual and lean-in to the issue of non-peace you felt. Is it still there? If it is, you may feel a slight contraction in your heart or elsewhere in your body. Record this in your journal. Then, do additional Remen Q̄ sessions. I suggest that you re-check the session work a few days later.

Breathing into Presence

Breathing into Presence after the initial three Remen Q̄ processes need only be redone when there is a significant break in the practice, for example, taking a class break or a lecture period of over 15 minutes.

You will only need to Breathe into Presence once at the start of your session after taking this class.

There is no harm done if you do it more often. Additionally, if the non-peace feels especially intense, I will do additional breathwork so I can focus.

Two More Rounds of Remen $\bar{Q}$

The teacher will guide you through two more rounds of Remen $\bar{Q}$ using the long command. This will prepare the students to start working with the IONS shortcut.

IONS (Intention, Origin, Neutralization, Snap)

If you have trouble with the original Remen Q̄ version being too long, you can use the IONS shortcut after completing the long version three times. After three times, you will have a body memory of the exercise. Then, you will be able to use the shorter method, IONS, instead of the longer version.

    I = Intention
    O = Origin
    N = Neutralization
    S = Snap

Shortcut Using IONS

After breathing into presence with eyes closed, replace the phrases with intention, origin, and neutralization.

1. **Intention** *(Say this in your inner voice.)*

2. **Origin** *(Say this in your inner voice and visualize a representation of the origin.)*

3. **Neutralization** *(Say this in your inner voice and visualize a change in the image. Halfway through visualizing the change, **snap** open your eyes.)*

4. Move your attention to your body and watch until you feel it is complete. *(If there is a sensation of lightness, swirling or bliss, allow the sensation to finish. The bliss may hang around a while.)*

5. Check in with your body and measure the non-peace intensity. Lean-in if necessary.

A Remen Q̄ session using IONS

The teacher will guide you through this exercise.

Ancestral Remen Q̄ Method

You may hold wounding in your DNA via epigenetic tags. *(See the Definitions chapter for further explanation of epigenetics.)* It may be challenging to know when to use this process. If you know that an issue stems from an ancestral issue, you can start with the Ancestral Remen Q̄ Process below.

If the non-peace is not epigenetic/ancestral, or if you have transmuted the ancestral influence and there is still something there, another origin will appear. You can then use the standard Remen Q̄ Method.

Step 1. Say in your inner voice with eyes closed: *I am witness to the field of intention to neutralize this field of information* (you continue to hold an awareness of the non-peace you are experiencing).

Step 2. Say in your inner voice with eyes closed: *I am witness to the origins of this created pattern in the field of information*. Then, visualize a DNA strand.

Step 3. Say in your inner voice with eyes closed: *I am witness to the neutralization of this created pattern in the field of information*. Then, create a shift in the visualization. Change the DNA strand into an image of your choice (sparkles, bubbles, pink dripping wax, dancing unicorns, a color, etc.).

Step 4. Snap your eyes open halfway through, changing the imagery. Then, focus your awareness on your body. Watch any sensations as they arise in your body. Stay focused on the sensations in your body until they are complete.

Do the body check-in to see if there is more work to be done.

Ancestral Method Practice

One of the enduring conversations I have had with people from around the world relates to the prejudices and the hatred one group has against another. These states of non-peace are endemic with humans, and in many cases, we have lost the historical context for these ancestral prejudices, but we have the epigenetics. Your ancestors may have escaped historical events of violence, famine, etc., and their fear kept it secret, even after they were safe in another country. There is also the possibility that an ancestor(s) was the persecutor and their guilt, shame or hatred, and the prejudice they would experience if their background were known kept them silent about their experience. They may have even lied about their country of origin. Recent developments in DNA testing have shown that to be the case many times.

For this next practice session, do you hold an ancestral wound that creates non-peace in your life today? Does your ancestry reflect a historical wounding? For example, a war(s), famine, forced religious conversion, colonization, forced into a boarding school, religious persecution, government persecution, genocide, enslavement, forced servitude, racial hatred, etc. Do any of your ancestors carry secrets? As you read this paragraph, did you feel a contraction or tightening anywhere in your body?

Do you resonate with any of the following:

- I can't throw away food (even if it is blue with mold).
- I can't throw anything anyway; I might need that someday.
- Change is dangerous.
- Life is hard.
- I must worry to stay safe.
- I must work hard to survive.
- No matter how hard I work, I can't get ahead.

- You can't make a living doing anything creative (being a writer, painter, etc.).
- I am prejudiced against _____ (this could be a cultural group, a country, a people, a religion, a racial designation, etc.).
- I hate _____ (this could be a cultural group, a country, a people, a racial designation).
- I cannot associate with those kinds of people.
- I will lose my family if I make friends with people different from me.
- Do you have a visceral or heart reaction to historical events when you first heard about them?
- I must take what the dead leave behind to survive.

There is a possibility that you did not resonate with any of the information above. If that is the case, do you have any ancestors who you perceive to carry the non-peace of those statements? If that is the case, then there is a possibility you carry an ancestral wound. Use that perception for this exercise.

Scripts

Scripts of Remen Q̄ sessions are given in this chapter. These are examples of work I have done on myself. The origin descriptions are often symbolic of the limiting pattern and are not necessarily an actual historical event.*

It is not necessary to see something. If you have trouble "seeing an origin", make something up; it will represent the vibrational frequency of the non-peace you are transmuting. Several people have commented to me that they use a single image for everything. This substitution works because you intend that the symbolic image represents the non-peace.

The scripts below were first published on the PeaceAlchemist.com website:

Remen Q̄ Script – Right Eye Cataract – feeling like nothing[5]

Recently, I started the journey of having new lenses implanted due to cataracts. After the surgery, I looked up what I had written about cataracts over 10 years ago in the Emotional Patterns database. The last emotional state resonated. I started the process by asking myself, "Do I feel like nothing"? My inner critic responded quickly, saying, "Yes, and you are nothing." My heart contracted, and the feeling was ancient. I have been doing this for a long time. For a long time, I have been numb to the intensity of that pain. My shoulders and neck tightened as I began the Remen Q̄. I did two separate rounds of breathing just to be more comfortable.

Right Eye Cataract Emotional State from Emotional Patterns
- Long-held ideas of being nothing have created a feeling of stagnation. Nothing is going to change, and nothing can be seen that would

---

[5] Moore, V. (2023). Remen Q̄ Script. Available from https://peacealchemist.com/remen-q-scripts.

change it. A feeling that they have been up against an incredible and overwhelming power and control that they cannot be present in. Their very existence produces fear, and they look down to exist in the energy of that control and fear.[6]

Session

Breathe into presence; I did this twice because of the intensity of the contraction.

1) First Remen Q̄
Intention Statement

Witness the Origin: A little kid is running (escaping) from someone with a stick. They are in an old hospital ward of cots, possibly in a war situation. They escape by hiding under the cots.

Neutralization Statement

Snap & Witness the Body

Body check-in: A lightness envelops my body. Heart feels neutral, still. There's tension in the shoulders and neck.

---

2) Second Remen Q̄
Intention Statement

Witness the Origin: Ancestral DNA method. DNA was in shades of grey, with what looked like snow on the rails. At the neutralization, the DNA pulled up from below, turned inside out and exploded.

Neutralization Statement

---

[6] Moore, V. (2018), Right Eye Cataract. Available from https://emotionalpatterns.com/cataracts-right/

Snap & Witness the Body

Body check-in: The heart is calm, and the shoulders are a bit less stressed. I asked if there was more and heard, "Yes."

---

3) Third Remen $\overline{Q}$
Intention Statement

Witness the Origin: Castaway as a sacrifice to save others. Found by a stranger and saved. Had been clawed by an animal.

Neutralization Statement

Snap & Witness the Body

Body check-in: The heart is much lighter. Shoulders indicate more work is needed.

---

4) Fourth Remen $\overline{Q}$
Intention Statement

Witness the Origin: At this point, I start asking questions. I moved my awareness into my shoulders and asked what was held there. I hear, "Lack of support. If you are nothing, you don't get support". At the origin vision, I am being beaten, and no one will help.

Neutralization Statement

Snap & Witness the Body

Body check-in: Heart is neutral and clear. My shoulders feel no stress, but I sense there is more to be worked on.

---

5) Fifth Remen Q̄
Intention Statement

Witness the Origin: There is a heaviness around the base of my neck, like a heavy collar, a heavy burden that is choking me.

Neutralization Statement

Snap & Witness the Body

Body check-in: Sleepiness takes over after energy quits moving through my body. My shoulders drop.

---

6) Sixth Remen Q̄
Intention Statement

Witness the Origin: Pretending to be asleep, avoid confrontation and possible abuse, feigned death.

Neutralization Statement

Snap & Witness the Body

Body check-in: Heart is calm and clear. I am relaxed, and my sleepiness has lifted.

At this point, I got up and left my study. It was nap time. As I lay down, I sensed that another round of Remen Q̄ was needed, and I set the intention to remember what had been the experience. When I got up from the nap, all my memories of what I had experienced were gone. I was complete.

If you resonate with this exercise, give yourself a couple of days and do the exercise again using the Ancestral Method.

Remen Q̄ Script – Benign Fasciculation Muscle Cramp Syndrome – feeling like nothing

About 3 years ago, I began to experience leg cramps 24/7. The cramps increased in intensity, and as the pain grew, so did my inability to walk any more than a few hundred feet in one day. The medical community took that long to hear me and prescribe something unacceptable. (Yes, I did transmute 'not being listened to'.)

This example is a long Remen Q̄ process consistent with a disease's crystallization.

Benign Fasciculation Muscle Cramp Syndrome, Emotional State from Emotional Patterns[7]

1. There's always another way. Too many directions pulling on them. They feel frustrated that all the different directions need their attention. Many demands overlap. Doesn't know how to get clear of the demands.
2. Wrong choices or just too many choices. Can't focus on what needs to be done now. Too many choices and no focus becomes no grounding. Afraid of selecting focus because they know they will be pulled in a more "needy" direction.
3. A loss of hope. No thoughts that things will change. A constant pulling away from taking care of self. Others become more important. Constant sacrifice and denial of their needs. Not allowed to feel the deprivation.
4. Hopeless. A deep sadness in their heart. Grief before grief. A narrowed life.

---

[7] Moore, Valeria (2025). Benign Fasciculation Cramp Syndrome. Available from https://emotionalpatterns.com/benign-fasciculation-cramp-syndrome/

Session
In this first session, I felt #4 Emotional State the most.

Start: Breathe into Presence

1) First Remen Q̄
Intention Statement

Witness the Origin: A long, sand-colored tunnel carved in rock. The tunnel appeared to go on forever.

Neutralization Statement

Snap and Witness the Body

Body check-in: Expansive movement, feeling a meditative high. Leaned-in → a subtle unease.

---

2) Second Remen Q̄

As I began, I felt a heartache.

Intention Statement

Witness the Origin: I am walking dusty streets in a dry place. I enter a door and sit down at a table. I am hungry, but there is no food.

Neutralization Statement

Snap and Witness the Body

Body check-in: Still a twinge of sadness.

---

3) **Third Remen Q̄**

   Intention Statement

   Witness the Origin: A gaunt woman dressed in rags comes out of the darkness.

   Neutralization Statement

   Snap and Witness the Body

   Body check-in: I felt a fleeting pain across my chest.

   ---

4) **Fourth Remen Q̄**

   There is a deep heaviness in my chest as I begin.

   Intention Statement

   Witness the Origin: A fellow stumbles into the scene. He is wearing loose white clothing, and he has been mortally wounded. He falls and tumbles down a cobblestone-paved incline.

   Neutralization Statement

   Snap and Witness the Body

   Body check-in: Neutral. But I need to look at this some more. There is a cramping in my left calf.

My attention is then pulled to Emotional State #1.

1) First Remen Q̄

Intention Statement

Witness the Origin: Image of many children making demands of me; they are crying. I hear myself say I have no strength to do this.

Neutralization Statement

Snap and Witness the Body

Body check-in: I feel a surge of energy through my body now. I still feel something. A feeling of flatness. Fleeting.

---

2) Second Remen Q̄

Intention Statement

Witness the Origin: I see an image of a woman in a long robe and gown coming down from a dusty hillside. A man runs up to her and says, "Neah, where have you been"? Many people have a sense of panic and desperately do not know what to do next. She appears to be amid a serious crisis with a group of people who follow her. As she enters the gathering, people grab at her robe as if it will bring solace and resolution. She was in a sacred place to get answers and direction. I levitated above the people. Their fear was too much.

I do not feel a heart contraction, but I know this is an issue for me. There is pain on the left side of my skull. At the base of my skull was a piercing pain. Now I have a headache all over.

Neutralization Statement

Snap and Witness the Body

Body check-in: I still have a bit of a headache.

---

3) **Third Remen Q̄:**

Intention Statement

Witness the Origin: I am pleading with god to save the people. They knew they were destined to die as I was. We were a lone group of sheepherders—good and quiet people. Yet we were to die.

I am triggered when too many needy people make demands on me.

Neutralization Statement

Snap and Witness the Body

Body check-in: Slight headache, but feeling calmer.

---

4) **Fourth Remen Q̄**

Intention Statement

Witness the Origin: A man walking a dusty road with a staff. A tall man with a grey beard. He feels defeated and as if he has failed. He does not want to go back to his home --- a person was unjustly accused and killed. He could not stop it. His name was Joshua.

Neutralization Statement

Snap and Witness the Body

Body check-in: My chest felt heavy as if something was pressing down on me.

My attention is now being pulled to Emotional State #3: I am constantly sacrificing and denying my needs. Not allowed to feel deprived.

My heart is contracting.

1) First Remen Q̄:

Intention Statement

Witness the Origin: A triggering violence, I will leave unwritten.

Neutralization Statement

Snap and Witness the Body

Body check-in: Tension in shoulders and neck. The crown at the suture lines is buzzing.

---

2) Second Remen Q̄:

Intention

Witness the Origin: Crossed hammer and pick image.

Neutralization Statement

Snap and Witness the Body

Body check-in: More relaxed, but still some tension at the base of the neck.

---

3) Third Remen Q̄:

Intention

Witness the Origin: Scene of violence.

Neutralization Statement

Snap and Witness the Body

Body check-in: Head pain gone. The tension at the base of the skull is gone. I feel peace, calm and neutral.

The muscle cramping ceased and has not returned. This exercise was done in December 2024. The muscle cramping turned out to be a symptom of something else instead of its own standalone malady.

Principles of Remen Q̄

a) Awareness
   i. It brings change into reality.
   ii. It brings you to the entire presence of the sensations in your body.
   iii. Focusing awareness on the body's sensations completes the shift to peace.

b) Ownership & Responsibility
   i. You change your identity by taking ownership and responsibility for your feelings as they apply to a non-peace relationship.
   ii. Ownership is taken when you take responsibility for creating a feeling of non-peace in a relationship.
   iii. There is no fault or blame in this process.

c) Breath
   i. Focuses intent
   ii. Focuses awareness
   iii. Mindful breath sets the intention for peace

d) Intention
   i. Produces the energy to change reality
   ii. When intention joins with desire, a flow of meaning is created.
   iii. Setting an intention creates a propelling force that energizes the Remen Q̄ process.
   iv. An intention for peace aligns with the probabilities that are the frequency of peace.

e) Witnessing Presence
   i. Allows for the observation to change in expanded awareness
   ii. Allows a deeper understanding of self
   iii. Is the soul's desire for the union of the minds

  iv. It is the potential for transmutation
  v. Is complete awareness without judgment
  vi. Allows for not reliving events and projecting
  vii. Allows for not needing the truth
  viii. Allows you to access the wisdom of a peaceful heart-knowing
  ix. Allows for possibilities that are blocked by judgment
  x. Is grace

f) Visualization
  i. Visualization is the inner process by which you observe a created pattern's vibratory representation and then witness the shift of that vibrational definition in your mind's eye.
  ii. Visualization brings awareness to the non-peace.

g) Neutralization
  i. A process of changing a relationship from non-peace to peace.
  ii. Neutralization is not a passive process; it is an active choice.

h) Transmutation of the Origin
  i. The visual you perceive represents the origin of the non-peace and visualizing starts shifting the non-peace to peace. By visualizing and setting the intention to neutralize the created pattern, you have acknowledged a pattern of non-peace. That acknowledgment has shifted the awareness of the pattern. That shift in awareness has started the transmutation to peace.

i) Awareness of the Body
  i. Completes the Remen $\overline{Q}$ process
  ii. With awareness, you are fully present to the sensations in your body
  iii. Snapping open your eyes disconnects you from the pattern of non-peace.
  iv. With awareness of your body, you are completing the shift to peace.

Rainbow Wrap

The rainbow wrap process is class-optional.

Over the last several years of working with Remen Q̄, there was one wounding that would not transmute. I would do the lean-in. It would appear to be gone, but it wasn't. In the years before Remen Q̄, I had explored this wounding with psychotherapy and many other modalities. This wound was not from this life but ancestral—a nexus point (see Definitions) or epigenetic. I found that this wounding would transform into a bypass after attempts to either transform or transmute. Within a few days or weeks, the heart-clenching wound was back. Finally, I sat with this and asked how I could transmute this non-peace. I then had a knowing of the process given below.

The Remen Q̄ process stays the same except for the origin visualization. In the origin visualization step, imagine the origin representation that causes unresolved guilt, shame, etc. or whatever symbol appears. Then,

   a. Imagine a rich brown light blanket wrapped around the origin visualization or symbol. It makes a cylinder shape. This blanket of light extends as far up as needed to encase the scene.
   b. Then, layer a red color of light wrapped on top of the brown.
   c. Then, layer an orange color light on top of the red.
   d. Then, layer a yellow color light on top of the orange.
   e. Then, layer a green color light on top of the yellow.
   f. Then, layer a blue-green color on top of the green.
   g. Then, layer a blue color light on top of the blue-green.
   h. Then, layer an indigo color light on top of the blue.
   i. Then, layer a lavender color light on top of the indigo.
   j. Then, layer a silvery white color light on top of the lavender. *(I know this is a lot of work. That is why it is only recommended when there is a recidivism in the wounding.)*

k. Then, bring in the Neutralization, AKA chaos (the changing of the origin and color blankets) and snap your eyes open at a halfway point.
l. Then, close your eyes and witness the energy shifts in your body. When you are complete, open your eyes.

Suggested Next Steps

1. Develop journaling skills if needed.

2. Continue or learn to meditate.

3. Expand your wisdom to other methods of transmutation: yoga, breathworks, tai-chi, Reiki, etc.

4. Expand your wisdom. For example, read about alchemical transmutation as a spiritual path. A beginner's article is one I wrote to be found at https://peacealchemist.com/my-alchemical-spiritual-journey/. For me, it was an acknowledgment of the path I was on. Read about hermeticism. Hermeticism is the spiritual foundation of alchemy. I also recommend the writings of Rudolph Steiner and Jiddu Krishnamurti. Visit a bookstore and let your curiosity guide you.

5. Learn to use your heart as a teacher. Your heart will contract when there is a wound.

6. Work with Remen $\bar{Q}$ as needed.

7. Subscribe to my YouTube channel. I am creating videos that pertain to your Inner Peace Journey
      https://www.youtube.com/@valeriamoore .

8. Learn Reiki. If you need a remote Reiki class, please let your teacher know or email me at valeria@valeriamoore.com and you will be provided with the name of a suitable teacher. Reiki is not just a healing modality. Reiki facilitates the opening of your third eye, reduces stress, promotes emotional healing and more. Reiki facilitates your transmutation.

9. If you have been on the Inner Peace Journey and have become a healer or a healing arts teacher, consider learning to teach Remen $\overline{Q}$. If you are considering teaching Remen $\overline{Q}$, purchase a copy of <u>Best Practices for Teaching Basic Remen $\overline{Q}$ and All Inner Peace Journey Work Courses</u>. Several more books are in the works that may provide the foundation for future workshops and teaching opportunities.

10. Sign up for my mailing list to hear about new classes and new books. You can sign up at https://peacealchemist.com.

11. As someone who has been on this path for a very long time, give yourself a rest from the path as needed.

12. If you feel like you need support, contact your teacher.

Conclusion

The Inner Peace Journey Work can seem endless. At times, the Inner Peace Journey can also seem pointless. The wounding you carry may seem without an end. And then there are times when a fire burns in your heart. Or you experience a peace so profound it is bliss. There is a longing for more information. You want to unwrap the mysteries of who you are. You want to heal. You want answers to the questions, 'What is the soul?' 'Why am I here?', 'What's my purpose?', 'Is there a purpose?'.

With consistent effort, you will begin to experience extended periods of inner peace. These times of inner peace will flow. You may even experience unbounded bliss. You may still experience emotional wounding and feel that familiar contraction in your heart or body, signaling a state of non-peace. But now you have the tools to move beyond the wounds. You are empowered.

Definitions

Akasha (Akashic Field, Akashic Records, Universal Mind) – The Akasha is a field of information that holds the memory of all that has occurred, will occur or occurs across all.

Aura – An aura is a field of energy that surrounds and interpenetrates the physical body of living things. Some traditions believe the aura reflects an emotional, physical, mental or spiritual state as a luminous emanation that can be perceived as a colored halo. The colors seen in the halo or field represent certain qualities. For example, a red light seen around the heart could mean anger is being held in the heart.

Beingness – Beingness is the flow of creative principles, manifesting as an awareness of self beyond identity. Our essence expresses the creative principle of memory and our choice in each moment.

Bypass – A bypass is a state where you believe you have released or cleared a state of non-peace and later discover that the change was temporary[8]. For example, you believe 'I am not good enough.' Perhaps you have used an emotional release technique to replace that created pattern with 'I'm good enough.' You believe that the created pattern has cleared, and then you discover that it returns the next time a trigger for 'not being good enough' is encountered. You may feel let down, disappointed, angry, betrayed, and untrusting if you have experienced a bypass. A bypass does not get to the underlying trauma that created the limiting pattern. A bypass does not get to the multiple traumas that are part of your experience of a limiting pattern.

---

[8] Moore, Valeria (2021). *The Remen Q̄ Method: An Easy Do It Yourself Process to Create Inner Peace and Change Your Reality*, pg. 75. Keizer, Oregon, USA; Three Moons Publishing.

A bypass may cause a person to be deceived into thinking that they can stop ongoing medical care. A bypass may mask symptoms of a serious chronic disease, thus causing a delay in treatment.

How do you know if you have set up a bypass? After transmuting a limiting pattern, lean-in or recall another example of the limiting pattern you are working on. When you lean-in, what do you feel in your body? What do you "see/feel/hear" in your inner vision/knowing? If you can still clearly visualize or feel the original limiting pattern, you have not completed the process. You will need to do more Remen $\overline{Q}$.

After you have transmuted the limiting pattern to peace and leaned-into the limiting pattern, recheck the limiting pattern after a sleep cycle to see if you have set up a bypass. The memory should have faded into a ghost-like shadow or a vague impression. Sometimes, you may have lost the memory of it altogether.

Chakra – There are many chakras in our subtle energy body (there are several schools of thought on how many). Chakras are energy centers in your body that correspond to bundles of nerves, major organs, endocrine glands and areas of your energetic body. The chakra receives, transmutes, and distributes prana, life force energy that energizes the physical body. The chakra receives a convergence of life force energy that flows through the nadis. The functioning of the chakras and nadis (energy channels that carry life force energy throughout the subtle body) is affected by the physical, mental and emotional bodies. The classical chakras (root, sacral, solar plexus, heart, throat, third eye, and crown) are associated with specific emotions that derive from the physical function associated with the chakra.

Creative Core - We are born with the ability to create and freely access inner wisdom, our creative core. Our creative core is the flow of inspiration and creativity from all of our bodies. We are born with transparent processes that allow us creativity and intuition based on physical, emotional, mental, and subtle body development.

Created Patterns (Beliefs) - A created pattern is a conceptual identification statement that underlies a behavior done over and over again. For example, a created pattern may be the ritual of drinking coffee first thing in the morning. The created pattern is identified as 'I must have my coffee first thing in the morning.' A created pattern may be feeling betrayed by "friends" repeatedly. The created pattern would then identify as 'My friends betray me.' This created pattern repeatedly tells a story of hurt and harm to prove a victim's status. The ritual of drinking a cup of coffee in the morning may not be limiting. However, the feeling and the created pattern of being betrayed by friends may have locked this person into a cycle of victim identity. This created pattern may be limiting.

The term "created patterns" reflects a shift from using the word' **beliefs**.' Words carry energy, and one of the aspects of the word 'belief(s)' is that it does not globally imply ownership. All 'beliefs' are patterns of creation by the individual holding them, regardless of the origin. Ownership, awareness of how their heart feels and the willingness to change a created pattern are essential if a person is genuinely committed to transmuting their state of non-peace.

The foundation of all limiting created patterns is fear(s). To stay safe, you adapt your life and responses to those patterns and create emotional states and multiple created patterns. The origin of fears, created patterns, and emotional states is not always from your life experiences. These limiting patterns may be passed down to you from your ancestry through either conception trauma, ancestral life experience or epigenetics.

Digging – Digging is a process of making assumptions or asking questions to find the origin of trauma.

Emotional Pathophysiology – "Patho" relates to disease and "physiology" is the normal functions of living organisms. Emotional pathophysiology looks at the physiological functions of an anatomical structure, for instance, the pineal gland, heart, spleen, etc., and what is emotionally held there at the functional level. Emotional pathophysiology is a deeper evaluation that gets to the root of the emotional patterns of disease. Emotional pathophysiology is pre-disease.

Emotional Release Therapy – Emotional release therapy is the generic term used to describe energetic processes that use a specific method of releasing stuck emotions or trauma that create dysfunction — examples: Reference Point Therapy, Emotional Freedom Technique, etc.

Emotional States – Emotional States is the term I use in my book, <u>Emotional Patterns</u>[9], to describe a set of vignettes of emotional wounds or trauma a person has experienced before getting a disease. Each disease can have multiple emotional states, fears, and created patterns.

The nature of all diseases is that we have had an experience and have not understood or learned the higher nature of the event. We have taken in the suffering and created an identity around the trauma. The value of emotional states is that they reference a conceptual grouping of created patterns within a vignette of behavior. Created patterns may be culturally biased in their wording and may not resonate with the person. For example, bowing to another person may be a sign of respect and honor in one country, but in another, it is considered an act of subservience. So, a set of beliefs around a physical act may differ across world cultures. The emotional state defines the evolution of fears and beliefs into behaviors that transcend the culture. Emotional states allow for translation into the respective value system. A person may resonate with all the emotional states, none, or an aspect.

Emotional States may have a masculine or feminine nature. The masculine or feminine nature does not mean a woman can have only the feminine or a man only the masculine. It means a person's feminine or masculine aspect reflects that emotional state. A person may be out of balance concerning the masculine or feminine aspects of self. For

---

[9] Moore, Valeria (2021). *Emotional Patterns: Fears, Emotional States and Created Patterns (Beliefs) by Disease, Disorder and Trauma Formerly Healer Wisdom Revision 1*. Keizer, Oregon, USA; Three Moons Publishing.

example, if the masculine is weak, they have many doubts. They doubt their abilities and capability to do things. There is a feeling of being intimidated by life, and moving forward is difficult. They fear putting themselves out there because they 'know' they will fail, so they don't even try to accomplish things. With a weak masculine side, one must show off attributes and accomplishments.

People with a weak feminine put a low value on others, and they do not give. There is a predisposition to be selfish, greedy, and closed off from people. Also, the weak feminine does not take responsibility for their actions but blames others for their problems.

An emotional state may hold many beliefs. Beliefs come together synergistically and create an amplified experience within the body. For example, a person has the created pattern 'I hate Aunt Edith.' Along with that belief, there is a reason for the hatred. Maybe the belief is based on the fact that Aunt Edith betrayed them. So, they believe 'Aunt Edith betrayed me.' Depending on the nature of the betrayal, the person may also believe that 'Women betray me.' All of the beliefs have a different vibrational quality that synergistically amplifies the energy of an emotional state. A single belief is limiting but may not produce a powerful shift. When different beliefs combine, the energy is amplified and the result may be disease.

The goal of the Emotional State information is to help you recognize a pattern(s) before the disease happens. Awareness of that pattern opens the door to begin a process of transmutation.

Emotional Wounding (may also be called 'wounding') – Emotional wounding results from a traumatizing or harmful experience (or set of experiences) that causes mental and psychological pain. Various traumatic, personal struggles or distressing experiences may cause these wounds. Trauma may include abuse (physical, emotional, or spiritual), neglect, loss of a loved one, accidents, witnessing violence, or any event that feels overwhelming and unsafe. Personal struggles may include chronic illness, financial difficulties, discrimination, and more. Distressing experiences may include betrayal, grief, rejection, bullying, or hurtful relationship experiences, such as living with a narcissist. The wound experienced over time or with significant intensity may cause different physical and energetic bodies to create a vibrational frequency representing a limiting pattern to become anchored in your body. The emotional wound will always affect the heart and different aspects of the body that resonate with the wound's vibration.

Epigenetics – Epigenetics is the study of inherited changes that are not changes to the genes. Instead, the inherited change affects how the gene is expressed. The change in expression is due to a chemical attached to the DNA. This chemical change, an epigenetic tag, may be inherited. For example, a person's ancestors may have experienced a severe famine and survived a bitter winter with very little food. The stress would have created epigenetic tags. Epigenetic tags are added to genes and affect how those genes are expressed. The grandchildren born to these ancestors will inherit the epigenetic tags that developed due to insufficient food and the fear of starvation. The grandchildren may live with the need to put away more food than is necessary. They may also experience anxiety around food.

Fears - At the core of every emotional state or created pattern (belief) is a historical trauma(s) or wounding. Historical trauma or wounding may come from your ancestry or a recent life experience. You frame your human experience of trauma within your familial, cultural, geopolitical, dogmatic or institutional rules. You may experience an instinctual response or fear if the trauma is physically threatening. That fear is then held in your mental, emotional and physical bodies. For example, you may have experienced severe food deprivation during a war. You may have experienced the fear of dying from starvation for a prolonged period.

After the war passed and food became readily available, you may continue experiencing the fear of dying from starvation. You may hoard food. You may feel like you never have enough food in your cabinets. You chastise those around you for wasting food. You may eat food your body does not need because you cannot bear seeing it go to waste. You may experience anxiety around events where food is abundant. Some of the fears being experienced are fear of dying, fear of being alone, fear of starving, fear of not having enough, fear of having food taken away, and more. These fears will play out in the different bodies. You may think (mental body) frequently about food: getting food, storing food, preparing food, eating, etc. You may feel anxious and worry (emotional body) about food. The anxiety and worry over time will crystallize into digestive and pancreatic issues (physical body).

Field – A field is a subtly defined multi-dimensional space of influence. If I say, 'I am witness to the field of intention,' I have made an intention with an area of influence. A relationship between two people would also be a field. The relationship occupies space and contains energy, creating an area of influence, a field.

Harmony – In a state of harmony, you experience the flow of the creative principle; you experience grace. When you flow with the river of life, the creative principle, you experience the knowing of our nature. Our essence expresses the creative principles of memory and our choices in each moment.

Heart-Soul Wisdom – This is the energetic bridge or portal between your intuitive heart and the Universal Wisdom/time continuum. This portal may be requested and activated for use. Universal Wisdom, when requested, will flow across this portal and into your awareness when you have reached the intersection of the Dancing with the Ego and the Self-Realization stage of intuition development.

Inner Peace Journey – The Inner Peace Journey is a lifelong process of seeking and cultivating inner calm and joy. Inner peace isn't a destination you reach, and you are done. It starts with a call from the heart. The heart feels a deep need to experience the infinite expansion of meditation, a spiritual practice, a connection to our divinity, to develop and know the wisdom of the ancients, to release the emotional energies that bind our hearts, and more. This journey may involve practices listed in the definition of Inner Peace Journey Work below and more. These practices facilitate the development of self-awareness, harmony, balance, and connecting with a sense of purpose.

Inner Peace Journey Work – Inner Peace Journey Work is a discovery process of understanding and knowing self. The wisdom of self leads to an understanding of the limiting patterns we hold: fears, limiting beliefs or patterns, traumas, thoughts, and potential motivations. That understanding is then used to transmute our emotional wounds using meditation, breathwork, journaling, bodywork, a spiritual practice, yoga, qigong, being in nature, art therapy, non-dualistic emotional transmutation work (Remen Q̄), etc. Inner Peace Journey Work brings you inner peace, greater creativity, increased self-awareness, improved relationships, and more.

Journey – A journey has an intentional focus set in non-local awareness that accesses information in a specific time, locale, and people.

Magical Thinking -- Relegates life's destiny to invisible superstitious forces for which you have no responsibility. Magical thinking may be how you coped with childhood trauma. The following are examples of magical thinking:

- When I win the lottery, all my problems will go away.
- If I lose five more pounds, my partner will love me.
- If I do what my husband tells me, he won't hit me again.
- If I am a better person, my partner won't get drunk.
- If I hear an owl hoot three times, I will die.
- If I ignore this problem, it will all go away.
- If I ignore this pain, it will go away.
- When I carry my crystal, no one will hurt me.
- My birth parents will show up someday and take me home.
- I must have my special necklace to stop bad things from happening.

Muscle Testing -- Muscle testing is based on the principle that your muscles will either strengthen or weaken in response to a statement. The muscles are tested for strength when a statement is made to determine its truth to you. One method involves pressing your forefinger and thumb together, and a healing practitioner holds your forefinger with one hand and your thumb with the other. As you make a statement, the healing practitioner will easily pull your fingers apart if the statement is false. Or, using both hands, you make interlocking circles with your thumb and forefinger pressed together; when a statement is made, you pull the fingers apart and break the circles. The supposition is that your muscles will weaken, and your fingers will pull apart easily if the statement is false. The problem is that fingers can develop diseases that weaken them, for example, arthritis. If your blood chemistry is out of balance, the muscle testing will be incorrect. If you are dehydrated, the muscle test will be inaccurate. If you are emotionally distraught, the muscle testing will be incorrect. Additionally, I have experienced people manipulating the test results. Several scientific studies have evaluated the validity of muscle testing, and the results indicated that muscle testing was no better than random chance.[10,11]

Nadis – These are subtle energy body channels, in conjunction with the chakras, carrying life force or prana throughout the body.

Nexus point – is an emotional wounding transferred from someone who is dying to someone who is touching them at the time of death. The emotional wound is then passed on to descendants.

A nexus is defined as a connection or series of connections linking two or more things, according to Oxford Languages.[12]

---

[10] Staehle, H. J., Koch, M. J., & Pioch, T. (2005). Double-blind Study on Materials Testing with Applied Kinesiology. *Journal of Dental Research*, 84(11), 1066–1069. Available from https://doi.org/10.1177/154405910508401119

[11] Unproven Diagnostic Tests. (n.d.). FoodAllergy.Org. Available from https://www.foodallergy.org/resources/unproven-diagnostic-tests

[12] Oxford Languages. 2025 Oxford University Press. https://languages.oup.com/google-dictionary-en/

The nexus point is a term you may not have heard before. Many years ago, I was working with a client using an emotional release modality, and the client had an issue that remained resistant to transformation. I decided to journey on the issue. I found myself witnessing a woman holding a man in her arms. The man was dying. At the moment of death, I watched as there was an energy transference that happened from him to her. The energy that was transferred held his anger, regret and a feeling of defeat at his being killed. I sensed that this woman was an ancestor of my client. The ancestor had taken on the emotional wounds from the man dying in her arms.

Past Life Regression – A past life regression uses hypnosis to access memories of a past life. Past life regressions may be used to access a past life that may be the source of trauma in the current life.

Trigger – A trigger is a connection or link to trauma from your current life or ancestry that provokes an emotional response. A trigger can be a physical item, a sound, a smell, an image, a color, a person's voice, etc. For example, you are standing in line at a store, and the woman in front of you is wearing perfume that reminds you of an aunt you loved. You are immediately overwhelmed with grief. That aunt passed away many years ago, and at that moment, you are overcome by sadness. The smell of the perfume was a trigger for your stuck grief.

Relationship – A relationship is a continuum of experience in space and time. A relationship is not a static feedback loop. Instead, a relationship is an energy flow between connected entities that continually creates your reality. You have many relationships. You have a relationship with people and things you know and don't know. For example, you have a relationship with a store clerk you see on Wednesday while grocery shopping. You may not know her name, but you have a relationship. Everyone who has touched your life has a relationship with you. You may not know the leadership of your country, but you have a relationship with them because they, directly and indirectly, influence your life. A relationship can also be non-human.

Example: When someone close to you dies, and you grieve their passing, you are grieving the change in the relationship.

Spiritual Bypass – A spiritual bypass is a defense mechanism that facilitates hiding behind a spiritual practice to avoid doing Inner Peace Journey Work. This practice has the effect of stopping your spiritual and inner growth. Below are some aspects of a spiritual bypass:

- Diverts and stops you from your inner work.
- You take shortcuts with your inner work and avoid dealing with difficult feelings. Doesn't engage in transmuting difficult emotions.
- Uses the phrase "you just need to let go" to dismiss the suffering of others.
- Uses metaphysical modality creations as a defense mechanism to divert from doing the hard inner work.
- Abrogates their ownership, decision making and responsibility to a metaphysical practice.
- Uses spiritual experiences to avoid the integration of spiritual wisdom.

Time Continuum – The time continuum is also known as the **Akashic Record, Universal Wisdom or Zero Point Energy field**. This field holds the vibrational frequencies of all that has or will happen in the All.

Transmutation – The definition from Merriam-Webster dictionary is to change or alter in form, appearance, or nature, especially to a higher form. In this book, Remen $\overline{Q}$ is used as a tool of transmutation. Remen $\overline{Q}$ moves you from non-peace to peace, a higher form of being, an elevated vibration. This elevated vibration is your natural state.

Trauma Response – A trauma response is the way we cope with traumatic experiences. [13]

Trigger – A trigger is a connection or link to trauma from your current life or ancestry that provokes an emotional response. A trigger can be a physical item, a sound, a word, a smell, an image, a color, a person's voice, etc. For example, standing in line at a store, the woman in front of you is wearing perfume that reminds you of an aunt you loved. You are immediately overwhelmed with grief. That aunt passed away many years ago, and you immediately feel overwhelming sadness. The smell of the perfume was a trigger for your stuck grief.

Universal Wisdom – The Universal Wisdom is also known as the **Akashic Record, Time Continuum or Zero Point Energy field**. This field holds the vibrational frequencies of all that has or will happen in the All.

Wounded Creative Core - The wounding of our creative core is the adaptation we made to survive institutional abuse. Institutions (schools, governments, familial, cultural and religious dogma) constrain the creative core and destroy inspiration, creativity and joy through shame, humiliation, rejection, shunning, violence and more. When a child experiences these controlling institutional tools, the creative core is wounded, and the creative flow is severely impaired. I have named this trauma the Wounded Creative Core. The Wounded Creative Core is a meta-state in many diseases.

---

[13] Trauma - Reaction and recovery. (n.d.). Better Health Channel. Retrieved March 15, 2024, from https://www.betterhealth.vic.gov.au/health/conditionsandtreatments/trauma-reaction-and-recovery

www.ingramcontent.com/pod-product-compliance
Lightning Source LLC
Chambersburg PA
CBHW081406070526
44583CB00020B/2693